ENGINEERING MARVELS
PALM ISLANDS

by Vanessa Black

poGo

Ideas for Parents and Teachers

Pogo Books let children practice reading informational text while introducing them to nonfiction features such as headings, labels, sidebars, maps, and diagrams, as well as a table of contents, glossary, and index.

Carefully leveled text with a strong photo match offers early fluent readers the support they need to succeed.

Before Reading

- "Walk" through the book and point out the various nonfiction features. Ask the student what purpose each feature serves.
- Look at the glossary together. Read and discuss the words.

Read the Book

- Have the child read the book independently.
- Invite him or her to list questions that arise from reading.

After Reading

- Discuss the child's questions. Talk about how he or she might find answers to those questions.
- Prompt the child to think more. Ask: If you had the chance to create an island in the shape of something, what shape would you choose? Why?

Pogo Books are published by Jump!
5357 Penn Avenue South
Minneapolis, MN 55419
www.jumplibrary.com

Library of Congress Cataloging-in-Publication Data

Names: Black, Vanessa, 1973- author.
Title: Palm Islands / by Vanessa Black.
Description: Minneapolis, MN: Jump!, Inc., [2017]
Series: Engineering marvels | Audience: Ages 7-10.
Includes bibliographical references and index.
Identifiers: LCCN 2017006797 (print)
LCCN 2017009931 (ebook)
ISBN 9781620317037 (hard cover: alk. paper)
ISBN 9781624965807 (e-book)
Subjects: LCSH: Artificial islands—United Arab Emirates—Dubayy (Emirate)—Juvenile literature.
Coastal engineering—United Arab Emirates—Dubayy (Emirate)—Juvenile literature.
Dubayy (United Arab Emirates: Emirate)—Juvenile literature.
Classification: LCC GB472.5.A78 B53 2017 (print)
LCC GB472.5.A78 (ebook) | DDC 627.98095357—dc23
LC record available at https://lccn.loc.gov/2017006797

Editor: Kirsten Chang
Book Designer: Molly Ballanger
Photo Researcher: Molly Ballanger

Photo Credits: Nikada/iStock, cover; Philip Lange/Shutterstock, 1; Evannovostro/Shutterstock, 3; Tatyana Vyc/Shutterstock, 4; Marat Dupri/Shutterstock, 5; Siegfried Layda/SuperStock, 6-7; Caro/Sorge/Newscom, 8; Kiev.Victor/Shutterstock, 9; Frank De Luyck/Getty, 10-11, 12-13; Alain BENAINOUS/Getty, 14-15; ASK Images/Alamy, 16-17; Yann Arthus-Bertrand/Getty, 18-19; GlobalVision Communication/GlobalFlyCam/Getty, 20-21; Photo travel VlaD/Shutterstock, 23.

Printed in the United States of America at Corporate Graphics in North Mankato, Minnesota.

TABLE OF CONTENTS

CHAPTER 1

NEW ISLANDS

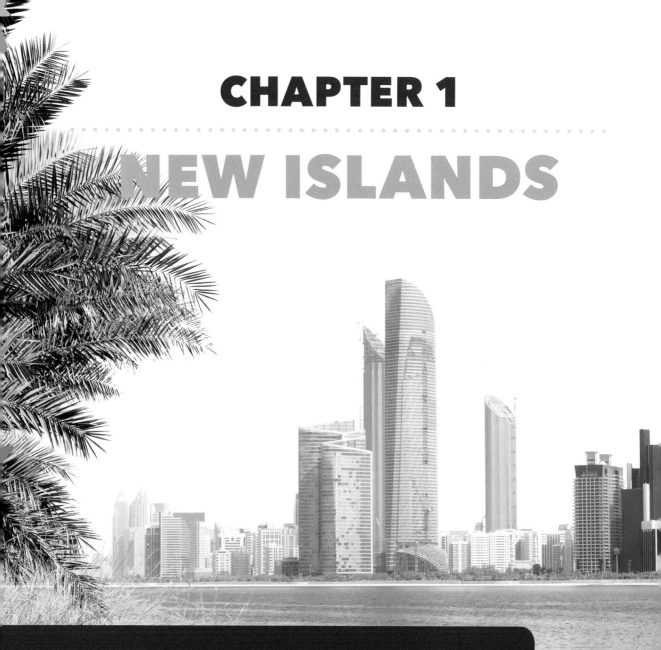

Dubai is a beautiful place to visit. This city in the Middle East has white beaches. It has clear blue water. The days are sunny and warm.

It is also home to an engineering marvel. The Palm Islands!

The Palm Islands are man-made. They are made from only sand and rock. There are three: Palm Jumeirah, Deira Island, and Palm Jebel Ali.

Before the Palm Islands, Dubai only had 45 miles (72 kilometers) of **coastline**. The **Crown Prince** of Dubai knew more people would visit if there were more beaches.

WHERE ARE THEY?

The Palm Islands are in the Persian Gulf.
The outer two are still being built.

PERSIAN GULF

Deira Island

Palm Jebel Ali

Palm Jumeirah

DUBAI

■ = Palm Islands   ■ = Persian Gulf
■ = United Arab Emirates

CHAPTER 2

DESIGN PLAN

The prince had an idea.
He would make more beaches.
How? By making islands.

They would have hotels, shopping malls, and homes.

Engineers planned. The islands had to withstand waves. They had to be strong enough to build on. They could not wash away in a storm.

They began building the first island in 2001.

CHAPTER 3

MANY CHALLENGES

First, they built a wall with sand and rock. This was the **breakwater**. It would protect the island from waves and **currents**. It would rise 10 feet (3 meters) above the water.

They needed a lot of rock. They needed about as much as it would take to build two Egyptian pyramids!

Each rock was placed by cranes floating on the water. All the rocks had to **interlock**. Each one weighed about six tons (5.4 metric tons)! Divers made sure they were sturdy.

breakwater

TAKE A LOOK!

The breakwater was built in sloping layers. This helps stop waves.

1. big rocks
2. small rocks
3. sand
4. seabed

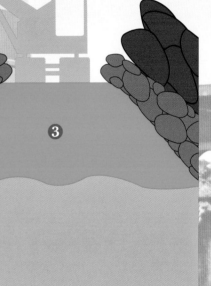

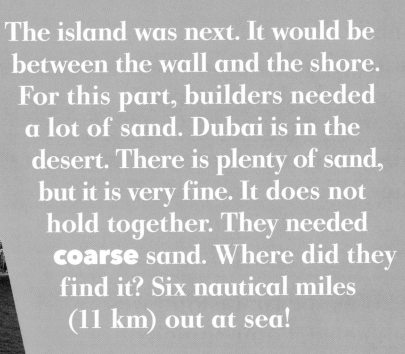

The island was next. It would be between the wall and the shore. For this part, builders needed a lot of sand. Dubai is in the desert. There is plenty of sand, but it is very fine. It does not hold together. They needed **coarse** sand. Where did they find it? Six nautical miles (11 km) out at sea!

Dredges scooped sand from the sea floor. Then they shot it through hoses. This is called rainbowing. They used **GPS** to make sure the sand landed in the right place.

DID YOU KNOW?

Dredges sprayed the sand at 33 feet (10 m) a second. That could fill a swimming pool in four minutes!

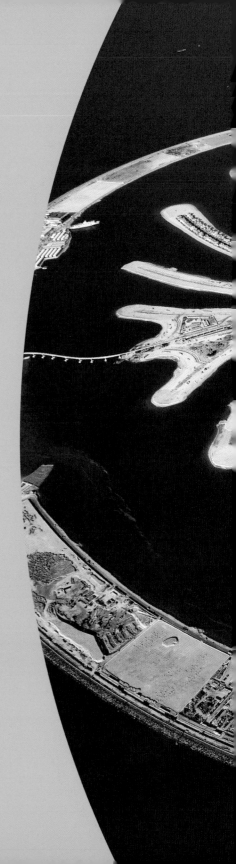

Finally, the island took shape above the water. Workers had to **compact** the sand. Cranes pushed tubes into the sand. They vibrated and added more sand. This made the land sturdy to build on.

In 2006, the first island was completed. Palm Jumeirah adds 35 miles (56 km) of coastline to Dubai. It is shaped like a palm frond.

The other two islands were started in the same way as the first. But they are not finished. When they are completed, they will be even bigger than the first island.

The Palm Islands are an engineering marvel!

ACTIVITIES & TOOLS

ISLAND EARTHQUAKE

The Palm Islands had to be designed to withstand earthquakes. How can an earthquake make an island disappear? Find out in this activity.

What You Need:
- large plastic bowl
- fine sand
- plastic bag
- 2-liter bottle
- water

❶ Put the sand in a plastic bag.

❷ Hold the sand bag about a foot (0.3 m) above the plastic bowl. Slowly pour the sand into the plastic bowl.

❸ Fill bottle with water.

❹ Pour water into bowl from one edge until half of the sand is submerged and an "island" forms.

❺ Simulate an earthquake by shaking the bowl back and forth gently. What happens?

❻ Small islands can disappear when earthquakes shake the ground. Earthquakes make the sand move. The sand compacts. It pushes the water up. This makes the sand act like a fluid. This is how an island can "sink" into the sea.

GLOSSARY

breakwater: A wall that is built in the sea to protect something from waves.

coarse: Made up of large pieces.

coastline: The land that is on the edge of the ocean.

compact: Firmly pack together.

Crown Prince: The son of a king or queen, who is expected to become the next king.

currents: Continuous movements of water within a body of water.

dredges: Boats that are equipped to remove sand from the bottom of the sea.

Dubai: A city in the United Arab Emirates, located on the southeast coast of the Persian Gulf.

engineers: Scientists who use math and science to solve problems and create things that humans use.

GPS: Global Positioning System, a system that uses satellites to find location.

interlock: Fit firmly together.

INDEX

TO LEARN MORE

Learning more is as easy as 1, 2, 3.

1) Go to www.factsurfer.com

2) Enter "PalmIslands" into the search box.

3) Click the "Surf" button to see a list of websites.

With factsurfer, finding more information is just a click away.